THE SMART KID'S GUIDE TO

Friendships

BY M. J. COSSON • ILLUSTRATED BY RONNIE ROONEY

Published by The Child's World®
1980 Lookout Drive • Mankato, MN 56003-1705
800-599-READ • www.childsworld.com

Acknowledgments
The Child's World®: Mary Berendes, Publishing Director
Content Adviser: Philip C. Rodkin, Professor of Child
Development, Departments of Educational Psychology and
Psychology, University of Illinois
The Design Lab: Design
Red Line Editorial: Editorial Direction
Amnet: Production

Photographs ©: Shutterstock Images, cover, 1; Shutterstock
Images, 5, 6, 7, 8, 11, 12, 14, 18, 19, 23, 25, 27, 29; Vika
Rayu/Shutterstock Images, 9; Denis Kuvaev/Shutterstock Images,
15; Aaron Belford/Shutterstock Images, 16; Darrin Henry/
Shutterstock Images, 21; Diego Cervo/Shutterstock Images, 22;
Martin Novak/Shutterstock Images, 26; Crystal Kirk/Shutterstock
Images, 28

ISBN 9781626873421
LCCN 2014930681

Printed in the United States of America
Mankato, MN
July, 2014
PA02224

ABOUT THE AUTHOR

M. J. Cosson was born in Des Moines, Iowa. She has been a teacher, writer, editor, and artist. She is a court-appointed special advocate for children in foster care. She has five grandchildren and lives in the Texas hill country with her husband and pets.

ABOUT THE ILLUSTRATOR

Ronnie Rooney took art classes constantly as a child. She was always drawing and painting at her mom's kitchen table. She got her BFA in painting from the University of Massachusetts at Amherst and her MFA in illustration from the Savannah College of Art and Design in Savannah, Georgia. Ronnie lives on a U.S. Army base with her infantryman husband and two small children. Ronnie hopes to pass on her love of art and sports to her kids.

CONTENTS

CHAPTER 1

What Is a Friend?

A friend is a person you like. A friend is also someone you trust. A friend is someone you want to spend time with. Some friends are a lot like you. Some friends are very different from you.

There is a saying about having friends. It goes like this:

There are three kinds of friends:

1. A friend for a reason
2. A friend for a season
3. A friend for a lifetime

What do you have in common with your friends? Do you have friends who are different from you?

Some people are friends because they do activities together.

A friend for a reason might be someone who shares an interest with you. Maybe you both love baseball. Maybe you're often in the same math or spelling group. Perhaps one of you is better at something than the other. You help each other in some way. Because of something that you share, you are friends. Can you think of someone who is a friend for a reason?

A friend for a season is someone you are friends with for only a certain time. It might be someone from your kindergarten class. You sat next to each other in first grade. You also shared your second grade classroom. In third grade, your friend moved away. Maybe your interests changed. You both made new friends. Most people have many friends for a season in their lives.

Sometimes friendships only last while you're in class together.

Some people will be your friends for most of your life!

A friend for a lifetime is special. You might already have a lifetime friend you've known since you were younger. Or you might meet a friend in sixth grade. You and that person could end up being friends until you are very old. Of course, you can't know which friends will be lifetime friends. When you are old, they will be special. They will have known you through your whole life. Think of a good friend. Can you picture yourselves as older together? It might happen!

All of these friends are important. When you make a new friend, you don't know how long the friendship will last. Some friendships will last your whole life. But some friendships will eventually end.

Knowing your own likes and dislikes can help you be a good friend. Friends often share an interest. A person who likes art might choose a friend who also likes art. A person who likes to play games might have the most fun with another game player.

Think about what you like. What are your favorite things to do? Do you like quiet or do you love to talk? Do you like to be outdoors or indoors? You might want to make a list. Many of the friends you make and keep will like some of the same things you do.

CHAPTER 2

Finding and Making a Friend

Sometimes you might feel alone. You might think everyone else has a friend and you don't. There are many reasons this might happen. But you don't have to keep feeling this way.

When you move to a new school district, you probably don't have friends. It's hard being the

*Playing alone is okay sometimes, but most people
want to be with friends some of the time.*

new kid. You don't know anybody. Everybody else
has a friend. Some kids seem to have lots of friends.

Maybe you're not the new kid. Maybe you've
always gone to the same school. Perhaps your best
friend moved away. Maybe you haven't found a
good friend yet.

Try joining in games on the playground. You might make a friend!

You might think that nobody wants to be your friend. The truth is that you are not alone. Other kids feel that way, too. You can talk to an adult at school or at home about friends. Sometimes an adult you trust can help you understand what you need to do to find a friend. An adult can also help you learn to be a good friend.

Whether you're new or not, don't worry. Most likely there are other kids looking for friends.

And who said a kid could only have one friend? A kid who already has friends might like to have you for a friend, too. Some of your friend's friends might become your friend. Soon you'll have lots of friends.

How do you find a friend? Look around on the playground. Is anybody out there alone? If so, go say hi. Is a group playing a game you like? Ask if you can join them. Most kids are friendly when they know you are, too.

There are many reasons a friendship works. Here are a few:
1. You like to do the same things.
2. You have the same talent.
3. You spend a lot of time together.
4. Your friend makes you feel happy. That's a great reason to be friends!

Try talking about things you have in common.

A **conversation** is a good way to start a friendship. To have a conversation, you need to make connections. For example, the other person has said, "I like to roller-skate." You could say, "I went roller-skating with my cousin. I fell down." Then the other person might ask if you were hurt. You could say, "No. In fact, I'd like to try roller-skating again." Your friend might say, "Okay, let's go!" That first conversation could be the beginning of a friendship.

Paying a **compliment** can help start a friendship. A compliment not only makes someone feel good about herself. It also makes her feel good about you. You said something nice to her. A compliment helps the other person know you care about her.

What might make someone notice you? A smile and a friendly "hi" can work. Most of the time, the other person will smile back. Next, think of something more to say. A question is always a good opener. Try to ask a question about something you can talk about, too.

Sharing is a good way to make and keep friends, too.

Being kind is another good way to make a friend. There are many ways to be kind. You could help someone who got hurt walk to the nurse's office. You could let someone borrow your eraser. You could hold the door. You could pick up something somebody dropped. Look for ways to be kind to others. A small kindness can tell people you would be a good friend.

People like to have different numbers of friends. Some people like to have lots of friends. Having one good friend is perfect for other kids. There's nothing wrong with either of these choices. How many friends would you like to have?

Here are two more ways to make a friend.

- Ask your family if you can invite someone over to your house. Maybe your new friend can stay for a meal.

- Clubs and teams are great places to make friends. It helps when you share interests and activities. If you like to play games, the school might have a game-playing club you can join. If you like to sing, a choir might be a good place to meet other kids.

For some kids and adults, starting a conversation with a stranger is hard. You can try practicing having conversations with someone you trust. The dinner table is a good place to have conversations. Or go on a walk together and talk.

Friends can be alike, or they can be different from each other.

Don't limit yourself to friends who are just like you. Look for friends who are different from you, too. You could choose friends who are girls if you're a boy—or the other way around. Or maybe your friends are from a different **culture** or background. Friends who are different make life more interesting.

You cannot make someone be your friend. Maybe you tried smiling and being nice to someone. You invited that person to come play. You have asked an adult for help. You have done all that you can do. However, if the other person is not interested, you must let it go. Not everybody wants to be a friend. This is a hard lesson to learn.

But there are other kids out there who would like you for a friend. Don't get **discouraged**. Keep that smile on your face.

Some kids say unkind things about others. They might even hurt others. Some kids are bullies. Use your good sense. Remember that this is not how friends act. If you are having problems with bullying, talk to an adult.

CHAPTER 3
Being a Friend

Caring about your friend is a huge part of true friendship. Part of being a good friend is understanding how your friend feels. If your friend is sad, you want to cheer him up. If your friend is sick, you want her to get better soon. If your friend just won an award, you are happy for him. It's time to celebrate!

A good friend knows how to control her temper. Your friend might do something that upsets you.

What if you fell down? You didn't get hurt, but you looked funny when it happened. Your friend couldn't help herself. She laughed at you. She said she was sorry, but it was too late. You were embarrassed. You were mad. What would you do?

You might stomp off and not speak to your friend. As a good friend, though, you would feel **empathy** for your friend. You would realize that she is sorry she laughed. You would accept the **apology**. You might even realize how funny you looked and laugh a little, too.

Saying you're sorry can end a fight.

Being a friend is like being on a team.

A good friend knows how to **cooperate**. You might **compete** with your friend in a sport or game. But competing is not the way of friends in real life. When you cooperate to get things done, you are acting as a team.

Here are some **qualities** of a good friend. These are qualities you want to look for in a friend. They are also qualities you can work on in yourself.

1. Interesting
2. Kind
3. Honest
4. **Loyal**
5. Funny

What qualities would you add to this list?

Practice empathy. Look in your friend's eyes. Look at her expression. Try to understand how your friend is feeling by looking at her. Put yourself in your friend's shoes. Try to feel like she is feeling. Then talk with your friend about how she is feeling. Ask what you can do to help.

CHAPTER 4

Losing or Keeping a Friend

Friendships end for lots of different reasons. It's sad when a friend moves away. When you really like somebody, it's hard to see him or her leave. There are things you can do to continue the friendship. You can talk on the phone or online sometimes.

Maybe you move often to a different town or school. If so, you might have done one of two things. You might have quit making friends because you know you will have to give them up when you move.

Or you might have figured out how easy it is to make new friends. If so, good for you! You have realized that a friend for a season is better than no friend at all. You can still have longtime friends as pen pals. And if you have learned to make new friends, you have a skill that will serve you all your life.

Some kids have pen pals. They are friends who write letters or send e-mails to each other. A pen pal is good for many reasons.
1. You get to keep your friend if one of you moves.
2. You can contact your friend any time you want.
3. You get to know about life in another place.
Some pen pals write for years. They might even meet again when they are older.

Sometimes you can save a friendship after a big fight.

It's really hard when a good friend doesn't want to be friends any longer. There are many reasons this happens. Perhaps you said something that hurt your friend's feelings. First think about how you might make up. Do you need to apologize? Do you need to admit that you were wrong? You might need to decide if a disagreement is worth losing a good friend over. Many people find that repairing a hurt friendship makes it stronger than ever.

Sometimes it's just time for a friendship to end. This might happen for all kinds of reasons. You or your friend's interests might have changed. You both have made other friends. Maybe you don't trust your friend anymore.

When friends grow apart, they often both know it is happening. Both friends might find new friends. Over time, you will see each other less. Keep those good memories. Sometimes an old friend shows up later in life.

As your interests change as you get older, you may lose old friends and make new friends.

Good friends stick together!

A true friend sticks around during tough times. Your friend might have done something that was embarrassing. Maybe your friend said something in class that he shouldn't have said. Everyone heard it. This might make you feel embarrassed. Other kids might not want to be around him anymore. You must make a decision. Will you stick by your friend? Are you worried that others might not like you if you stay friends? Will you end the friendship?

These are difficult questions! It can help to talk it over with an adult.

As you continue to grow, you'll get better at making and keeping friends. You will have had more experience at friendship. It's part of growing up. You might keep the friends you have now. You will make new friends, too. If you are a good friend, you will do both. Having good friends is one of the biggest joys of life. It's worth it to be the very best friend you can be.

Think about what makes you happy. Chances are, it makes your friends happy, too!

TOP TEN THINGS TO KNOW

1. Be honest and trustworthy to your friends.
2. Know your strengths, so you know what you bring to the friendship.
3. Smile and start a conversation.
4. Show a friend that you care with kind words and thoughtful acts.
5. Try to look at things from your friend's point of view.
6. Understand that your friends are different from you.
7. Stay in touch if you move or your friend does.
8. Talk to a trusted adult for friendship advice.
9. Apologize if you hurt a friend's feelings.
10. Be loyal to your true friends, even when they embarrass you a little.

GLOSSARY

apology (uh-PAH-luh-jee) An apology is words or actions that say you are sorry. Making an apology after a fight can help make things better.

compete (kuhm-PEET) To compete is to try to do better than someone else. People compete in sports but don't need to compete in friendships.

compliment (KAHM-pluh-munt) A compliment is something nice that someone says about another person. Paying a compliment can make your friend happy.

conversation (kahn-ver-SAY-shun) A conversation is talking with another person. Have a conversation to get to know someone.

cooperate (koh-AH-puh-rate) To cooperate is to act with others to get something done. Cooperate with your friends.

culture (KUHL-chur) Culture is the customs and ways of life of a group of people. People from a different culture might celebrate different holidays than you do or wear different clothes.

discouraged (dis-KUR-ijd) Being discouraged is feeling unsure or having less confidence. Don't be discouraged if you don't make friends right away.

empathy (EM-pah-thee) Empathy is the awareness and sharing of another person's feelings. You can practice empathy so you can be more helpful to your friends.

loyal (LOI-uhl) Someone who is loyal is faithful or a strong supporter. Good friends are loyal to each other.

qualities (KWAH-li-tees) Qualities are ways of being. Some qualities are shyness, intelligence, and courage.

BOOKS

Cohen, Miriam. *Best Friends*. New York: Aladdin, 2007.

Greive, Bradley Trevor. *Friends to the End for Kids: The True Value of Friendship*. Riverside, NJ: Andrews McMeel Publishing, 2006.

WEB SITES

Visit our Web site for links about friendships:
childsworld.com/links

Note to Parents, Teachers, and Librarians:
We routinely verify our Web links to make sure they are safe and active sites. So encourage your readers to check them out!

INDEX